CONSERVATION
NATION
PRESENTS:

CONSERVATION NATION

Through My Anacostia Eyes:

Environmental Problems and Possibilities

Contributions by UDC-DOI Justice 40 Internship Students and Staff

Edited by Caroline Brewer

Printed in the United States of America

Through My Anacostia Eyes:
Environmental Problems and Possibilities

INTRODUCTION OF PARTNERS

PARTNERS IN THE ANACOSTIA 2023 SUMMER INTERNSHIP PROJECT

Conservation Nation

At Conservation Nation, we are working to save wild animals, their habitats, and our planet by building a more inclusive conservation movement. By investing in future leaders from underrepresented communities through education, career development, and funding, we are creating opportunities to bring more voices and more solutions to the urgent biodiversity challenges facing our planet. We believe that all students deserve equitable access to inspiring role models and fun experiences in nature. We were honored to support nature-based field trips and bring Caroline Brewer and her Nature-Wise Literacy and the Environment Program to Anacostia High School students as part of this summer internship program.

Diane Lill, Education Director

Diane Lill (right) is the leader of this initiative for Conservation Nation. She has been assisted by Joanna Levi (left), Associate Director, Education & People, and Miguel Zarate, intern.

Consultant Caroline Brewer and Nature-Wise

Nature-Wise helps us explore and connect with the natural world, our place in it, and our power to better protect all living things. We help students understand and practice, on creative levels, that human beings are also included in the definition of the environment. We, too, are nature and from our earliest days, we practice literacy. Nature-Wise is a professional development program and a series of workshops for students that uses literature, including tons of children's literature, videos, and literacy activities to support students in expressing themselves as readers, writers, speakers, song-makers, and storytellers, in general. They get to explore and evaluate wildlife (colors, shapes, patterns, textures, and behaviors of plants, animals, waterways, and humans) in their neighborhoods and beyond. For this summer program we wanted to support the students in making this book, *Through My Anacostia Eyes: Environmental Problems and Possibilities.*

Caroline Brewer is the creator of Nature-Wise, a professional speaker, trainer, environmentalist, literacy activist, consultant, and author, most recently, of the picture book *Say Their Names.* She is the former Chairwoman of the Taking Nature Black Conference, co-founder of Black to the Future Nature Alliance, and former Marketing and Communications Director of the Audubon Naturalist Society. She is currently working on national and international forums to address climate change and other environmental crises and writing children's books about nature.

The University of the District of Columbia (UDC)

The University of the District of Columbia (UDC) is the only public institution of higher learning in, and for, the nation's capital. UDC is a Historically Black College and University (HBCU) and the only exclusively urban land-grant university in the United States. In alignment with this unique position, UDC has established the Developing America's Workforce Nucleus (DAWN) STEM talent pipeline initiative as a key strategic priority. DAWN includes a partnership with the Department of Interior and other District and federal partners to operate a six-week high school student internship program at Anacostia High School focused on creating multi-credential, seamless STE(A)M academic and career pathways for Black, brown, and economically disenfranchised students. Patrick Gusman, Deputy Chief of Staff, is the leader of this initiative for UDC.

Xavier Brown

Xavier Brown is the Coordinator of the UDC - DOI Justice 40 Internship and the Anacostia Ambassador Director in the Office of the President for UDC. Brown is UDC's "boots on the ground," supporting the environmentally-focused Anacostia High School Redesign and driving UDC's overall education partnership efforts with the Department of Energy and Environment (DOEE), the schools in the Anacostia High School feeder pattern and other schools in Ward 8, the District of Columbia Public Schools (DCPS), and community leaders and residents in Ward 8. Brown will also serve as Anacostia Ambassador in the Urban Waters Federal Partnership (UWP). The UWP is a nationwide program with partnerships in 20 different cities around the U.S. and the Anacostia River.

The Department of the Interior/The National Parks Service

The Department of the Interior (Department) plays a central role in how the United States stewards its public lands, increases environmental protections, advances environmental justice, and honors our nation-to-nation relationship with Tribes. The Department's Office of Environmental Policy and Compliance (OEPC) serves as a leader in resource stewardship and the sustainable and equitable management of the Department's resources. We foster partnerships to enhance resource use and protection as well as to expand public access to safe and clean lands under the Department's jurisdiction. We strive to continually improve environmental policies and procedures to increase management effectiveness and efficiency. The National Park Service's Stewardship Institute is actively engaged in keeping the National Park Service at the leading edge of stewardship for our natural and cultural heritage and is supporting OEPC in developing innovative partnerships to support underserved communities.

Courtney Hoover, Carly Buta, and Rebecca Stanfield McCown are leaders for DOI/NPS in the UDC-DOI Justice 40 Internship Program.

ACKNOWLEDGMENTS

Alexis Allen.
Kahri Borum.
Dearontre (Dre) Daise.
Erica Doughty.
Royana Easterling.
Keveon Graves.
Dewand Hemsley.
NeKaeyla Roach.
Germaine Williams.
Marcus Williams.
DeMirio Wimbush.
Jeremiah Wright.

To each of you, we owe our deepest gratitude. For your presence, for your power, for your insight, your humor, your honesty, your hope, your help. For you being who you are: brilliant, magnificent, alive and eager to make your mark on the world. There would be no book without you. You are the primary storytellers -- the engines and the ingenuity of this work -- and it's through your eyes that we get a better view of the world and Anacostia. Thank you. I hope you will long celebrate your contributions to this new and unique work.

To UDC Deputy Chief of Staff Patrick Gusman and his team, including lead Summer Internship Coordinator and Anacostia Ambassador Xavier Brown (my dear colleague from the Taking Nature Black Conference) and the team at the Department of the Interior and National Park Service – Courtney Hoover, Carly Buta, Rebecca Stanfield McCown, Cheryl Kelly, and Ryan Hathaway, Director of Council on Environmental Quality for the Office of the President, please accept our deepest appreciation.

What a gift it has been to work with you. Together, your teams developed a robust set of experiences that took Anacostia students up and down the Anacostia River, through the park, to local and federal offices in the city, to gardens in schools, outside schools, and on rooftops. And you invited in a host of environmental professionals to share their knowledge and experiences with the students, and take their questions and feedback. I'm thinking there must have been at least 30 of these experiences over five weeks of the six-week program. Scheduling and keeping everybody on track was no small feat. Thank you for persevering. We couldn't fit all of those experiences in this book, but we know the students will hold the richness of every adventure in their heads and hearts for many years to come.

Thank you to Danielle Simmons, an Anacostia Ambassador and UDC intern, who was Xavier's right-hand woman, traveling with the students on most field trips, and leading their experiences in the gardens, teaching them the finer points of the climate crisis, encouraging and supporting them as writers, helping them develop their final presentations, and rescuing them with snacks on days when they weren't too pleased with the cafeteria's offerings. Trust me, the students were grateful!

Thank you to UDC interns Ayoub Mouchtahi, Toluwalase Adetosoyet, Allan Muir, Tukey Francis, Oqueive Horne, who also provided back-up on field trips and encouraged and supported the students as they reflected on their journeys in writing. This book would have taken even longer and been more challenging to produce without your help.

Thank you to Jacob Campbell, UDC Program Associate for Project Based Learning, and leader of the Hydroponics Lab program, and Assistant Olivia Howard, for giving the students nearly immersive experiences in the lab and sharing your story on video and in writing for the book.

A huge, ginormous hug and round of thank yous to Gabriela Paola Franco Peña, our book's designer and the photographer at Kenilworth Aquatic Gardens, for saying yes to this assignment, knowing it would require more hours -- including late nights and early mornings --than she signed up for. Huge thank yous for her integrity, her creativity, and her commitment to making the book not only something that the general public would enjoy, but that would make the students, and all the contributors, forever proud.

My deepest appreciation to Conservation Nation's Executive Director Lynn Mento, the board, Education Director Diane Lill, Associate Director for Education and People Joanna Levi, and Intern Miguel Zarate. Your enthusiasm for doing the intense work that it would take to make this book happen has been breathtaking and the source of so much joy. It's been a great privilege to be your partner in this endeavor and to witness your commitment to these students, and the stories they have to tell about the environment.

Special appreciation to the UDC Foundation and Pepco Holdings for covering the design expense and printing costs for the first printing of the book.

EDITOR'S NOTE
by Caroline Brewer

The leaders of Conservation Nation and I met earlier this year and agreed to work together on their big idea: a commitment to promote diversity, equity, and inclusion through our partnerships with schools and youth-serving organizations. Conservation Nation, which grew out of the Friends of the National Zoo, had re-imagined itself as a national leader in conservation, whose primary mission is to elevate underrepresented voices and cultivate relationships that invest in the environmental champions of today and tomorrow.

As an author and literacy and the environment consultant, they had me at hello. And so did Xavier Brown when he invited us to be a part of the summer project, and so did Patrick Gusman and the DOI/ NPS team when they welcomed us with open arms.

Whatever progress we make protecting the environment we will make because we know that we need everyone. We need every voice, every hand, every heart, every soul, and every mind. The younger, the better. The more diverse, in every way, the better. So, with *Through My Anacostia Eyes: Environmental Problems and Possibilities,* we meant to take a small leap forward, to move the needle on this big idea, and watch for what more the universe will do through our earnest actions.

The Nature-Wise curriculum introduced students to ways of knowing about nature and the roles they could play in better protecting it through children's literature, research, and thoughtful reflections as group and individual writers. The goal was to encourage our young people to find their voices on these important matters and gain more confidence in sharing them. It was to help them begin to identify as capable thought leaders on conservation and environmental affairs, on anything and everything that affects their quality of life. And it was to help us learn from them, to see the environment through their eyes, their lived experiences. It was to provide a tool that would lift us all higher than we might have imagined. It was to build community, rich with possibility and promise. I am thrilled about what will unfold for all of us, and especially the young people, as the book makes its way around the world.

Whether these students explicitly choose careers in the field or not, their voices matter. They are residents, citizens, and members of the global environmental family. We need now and forever the benefit of their wisdom, wonder, and critiques. We are indebted to them for all the ways they helped us learn and grow this summer.

Please enjoy this book, and let us know how it affects you.

What You Don't Know by Looking at Me

What You Wouldn't Know by Looking at Me
by Royana Easterling

You wouldn't know I run track by looking at me.
I'm not as fast as a cheetah but I'm not as slow as a turtle.
I'm a perfect in between.
You wouldn't know I'm going to 10th grade by looking at me.
I don't look too young but I don't look too old either.
You wouldn't know my favorite food is chicken nuggets by looking at me.
You wouldn't know my favorite color is pink by looking at me.
You wouldn't know if I'm nice or not by looking at me.
You wouldn't know if I got friends by looking at me.
I like to be by myself but I don't like to be lonely, with no friends.

What You Don't Know by Looking at Me
by Keveon Graves

What you don't know by looking at me is that:
My favorite food is the potato because of the many ways it can be cooked --
fried, boiled, baked, and mashed, just to name a few.

What you don't know by looking at me is that:
My favorite sport is basketball, which would surprise most people as I am built like a football player.
While being 5'10 1/2" at 15, my biggest fear is heights.
I am a huge tech person, especially when it comes to phones, computers, and video games.
My preferred phone brand is a Samsung over an iPhone because Samsungs are more durable
and last longer than singing *Happy Birthday!*

What you don't know by looking at me is that:
My favorite subject is Math, both at home and school.
My dreams that I have while sleeping are sometimes better than the reality I face
while constantly awake.
I play video games more than I do anything else
and I use them to escape the pain of real life.

What you don't know by looking at me is that:
I was born in the summer and prefer the heat.
For my 4th and 5th grade years of school, I lived in Williamsburg, Virginia
at a predominantly white school.
My favorite color is blue, which isn't too much of a surprise because it's the color
I wear most often, other than black.
But my second favorite color is purple and I don't mind wearing it.

What you don't know by looking at me is that: My left hand writing goes well with my right-handed
jab and swinging arm. My left jab can be compared to Mike Tyson's.

What You Don't Know by Looking at Me
by Dearontre (Dre) Daise

I will start this story off by telling you who Dearontre Daise is.
I come from a family of eight. My parents have been teaching me right
from wrong since I was brought to life.
They steered me away from numerous tempting situations,
like stealing for fun.

What you don't know by looking at me is that I met a second father figure,
this man named Moe. His mentorship not only shaped my understanding of the game
of football, but also instilled in me invaluable life lessons. One of those lessons
was basically to stay away from the streets, stay away from things such as getting
involved with drugs or gun violence.

What you don't know by looking at me is that through Moe's unwavering support
and mentorship, he poured his wisdom into me, leaving an indelible mark.
He would go out of his way to pick me and my brother up from our house on 55th Street NW,
near Clay Terrace, after leaving his job at Children's Hospital, miles away, to make sure we got to
practice every day. To make sure we stayed clear of the streets.

What you don't know by looking at me is that Moe was very consistent in his desire
to see us win – on the football field and in the game of life. He taught us
that there's more to the world than DC. That we have to look ahead, beyond
the city. He taught us to not get stuck in our thoughts here. He was like a beacon of hope.

He taught us to follow through on our goals. It was like our goal to win the
Gray Bowl Championship. I'm a guard. Every block in every game was a commitment
to our goal to win the championship the same way every time I stayed away from
the streets was a commitment to my goal to succeed in life.

What you don't know by looking at me is that if Moe and I did not meet on that day,
the Dearontre you see today would be different.

What You Don't Know by Looking at Me
by Dewand Hemsley

What you don't know by looking at me
is that I'm the baby of the family.
My sister protects me like a mother bear
protects her cubs.

What you don't know by looking at me
is that I'm from a place where we have
more cookouts than people in North Carolina do;
where rappers don't rap on beat;
I'm from a place where I'm a young entrepreneur.

What you don't know by looking at me
is that I'm from a place where my mom
didn't want me to grow up; a place that I want
to make it out of; a place from where I want
to make it to the NFL.

What you don't know by looking at me
is that I'm from a place where I've lost friends
to gun violence; a place where bullets
don't have names on them.

I'm from a place called Washington D.C., Southeast.

What You Don't Know by Looking at Me
by Erica Doughty

What you don't know by looking at me
is that I don't like writing
because it's boring and is kind of pointless
because I have to explain everything
and my hand hurts.

What you don't know by looking at me
is that I don't like texting on a phone.
I also don't like reading
because staring at a spot
for too long
strains my eyes.

What You Don't Know by Looking at Me
by Erica Doughty

What You Don't Know by Looking at Me
by Jeremiah Wright

I'm Jeremiah Wright. That's one thing to know about me.
You're not going to know a lot by looking at me.
Some people may misinterpret who I am.
I say that because it has happened before.

What you don't know by looking at me is that
I am a Black boy from D.C., born and raised.
Growing up here is hard as a rock, but you'll see
a lot of motivation in my eyes.
On the outside, I might seem like the chillest
person in the world, but I'm also always so excited.

What you don't know by looking at me is that
I have a big family, so big that it seems it could
fill a football stadium. It's very confusing to explain,
so I won't.

What you don't know by looking at me is that
I am a quarterback at Anacostia High School.
I'm going to 12th grade I also play basketball.
I would say that I'm good. I would also say
that my family is athletic, but I think I'm different.
My abilities come from God, not genetics.

What you don't know by looking at me is that
I'm smart, caring, and loving.

What You Don't Know by Looking at Me
by Nekaeyla Roach

What you don't know by looking at me is that
I am the diamond that grew through broken concrete.
That means I got tough skin and I'm brilliant too.
I come from a neighborhood where
we don't know the difference
between fireworks and gunshots;
between what's supposed to be fun
and what's trying to kill you.

When I was a child, I would play outside,
running the streets with my hair all over my head.
On the Fourth of July,
I would always hear fireworks and see them fly.

One time, I stopped running,
turned around and looked back. I see everybody
dropping to the ground. Somebody yells out,
"Those aren't fireworks. Those are gunshots."
"Everybody get down!"
I'm going to wind up with a knot on my head,
I would think, because of how fast, how hard, I fell.

I am the diamond that learned the difference between
self-love and self-harm.
There's more to it than just hearing
"it's going to be okay" and cuts on your arm.
Loving yourself is saying no to things
you don't want to do.
Loving yourself is knowing how to always show up for you.
Self-harm is making choices that hurt you
and your self-development in the long run.
It's like shooting yourself in the foot
with your very own gun.

I love to refer to myself as a diamond, because of the
trauma, losses, hard times, and pressures I have survived.
You see, I'm still kicking and alive.
Pressure produces diamonds,
and knowing that I survived
everything that's been thrown at me --
really, it's what makes me strive.

I am diamond that grew through broken concrete,
walking through poverty
wondering if I'll have a dollar
for the next homeless person I see;
Looking for ways to help someone else,
not just me.

I am the diamond that always has the urge
to acknowledge, smile, and compliment
any stranger I come across.
On top of that, after my grandma's passing,
I'm still trying to get through that loss.

Living in Southeast DC, I think about my friends
from middle school being killed
and not making it to senior year.
The world I live in, you don't make it to 16,
and I know for a fact that's one of our biggest fears.

I am the diamond that wants to attend Spelman University
to become one of the best Black women lawyers as a career.

I want to rise to the top, so I know I can't stop
being the diamond that grew through broken concrete
because fulfilling my dream is near.

What You Don't Know by Looking at Me
by Marcus Williams

What you don't know by looking at me
is that I am a boy who wants to be free.
I am a summer baby that loves the winter.
I am an advocate for my community.

What you don't know by looking at me
is that I grew up with screaming and yelling
and being told to be a leader, not a follower.
So here I am.

What you don't know by looking at me
is that I am boy growing up in Southeast fighting
to make a change.
I am the yellow sun, a bright ray of light
who wants to be a geological mining engineer.

What you don't know by looking at me
is that I am a lefty who loves writing, loves reading,
Manga, and watching anime.
I am a boy who likes to chill
and be in the house all day.
I am a boy who loves video games and eating.

What you don't know by looking at me
is that I like water parks and hate roller coasters.
I am a boy who loves money and dreams
of having lots of it.
I am a boy who loves school, loves to learn
and nothing will ever change that.

What you don't know by looking at me
is that I am a boy who came from a dad that is proud of me
and who doesn't want me to be like him.

Once again, I am overall a boy who wants to be free.

What You Don't Know by Looking at Me
by Alexis Allen

What you don't know by looking at me is that I like staring at the moon at night.
The moon shines so bright that it almost looks perfect, as if I were staring at a diamond.

Everybody loves the moon. It reminds me of my favorite flower, a tulip or maybe a dahlia,
which is round and full of small petals.

Both flowers share the same beauty and that beauty reminds me of the moon.
I love the moon. I wish I could be the moon.

What You Don't Know by Looking at Me
by Germaine Williams

What you don't know by looking at me is that
I'm from a lady who was adopted and is a lone wolf.
I'm from a family where you hear arguments left and right.
I'm from a street where they light fireworks 24/7.
I'm from a place where we play video games a lot.

I'm from a place where I once reached the top 5 in my grade.
I'm from a place where I won 3rd place for ice skating.
I'm from a place where I'm the oldest of four children.
I'm from a place where I am who I want to be.

CHAPTER 2

My Superpower

My Superpower is Listening
by Marcus Williams

My superpower is being able to sit down and listen to another person. Everyone needs someone to just sit down and listen to their issues. So, therefore, I feel as though I help others by just allowing them to make their voices heard.

Allowing their voice to be heard means their words flow out their mouths and they never have to worry about the situation again. Allowing them to speak and let everything out allows for them to feel a sense of relief.

It's a feeling similar to when you're lying down on a patch a grass and you can feel the breeze.

My Superpower is to Be One with the Earth
by Germaine Williams

If I had a superpower, it would be to be one with the Earth, so that way I would be in communication with the Earth. That way, if there's to be an earthquake, I would be able to help others get to safety and I would be known as the Hero of the Earth.

My Superpower is the Ability to Avoid Conflict
by Keveon Graves

My superpower is the ability to avoid conflict. I am looked at by many, such as my friends, teachers, and even family members, as this "innocent" child who doesn't have problems.
However, I'm really not a fan of this persona all the time.
I am only viewed the way I allow people to view me.

If I want to be viewed as a violent person, then I would simply attack someone who I dislike, but I don't. For the most part, I don't like being part of drama, but if put in what feels like a "perilous" situations, I can go there.

I haven't been in life-threatening situations caused by other people.
If I'm in a situation where I feel like violence or aggression is being directed towards me,
I just stand down for my own protection; walk away or stop talking.

I know I can't always win, but I won't surrender in a battle that I know is possible to win.
I'm one of the smartest people that everyone I know knows.
My brain is a mansion that I won't allow to be broken into.

In the Gardens at Sousa, Kramer, and the UDC Rooftop:
Ripeness, calm, and a sea of green
A collage of conversations and written responses

Contributors: Keveon Graves, Dearontre (Dre) Daise, Erica Doughty, Dewand Hemsley, Germaine Williams, plus Xavier Brown and Caroline Brewer, Arranged by Caroline Brewer

I saw
the green, grown tops of the crops that had been planted, Keveon recalls.
In a picture,
wavy green leaves stretch for yards and yards in neat rows,
Ms. Caroline notes.

The kale - rough, wrinkly, like a 90 year-old man's face – was almost ready,
Erica says. The kale was green. Just green. Ordinary, she insists.
No, not lime green. Dark green, she persists, and notes that students tried the kale.

Keveon ate a tomato, Erica writes.
He says it was ripe, bright red, with flesh like a plum. About the size of a plum.
We were shocked, many students say, that some people were eating out of the garden
without washing off the food.

Why do you think they did that?, Ms. Caroline asks.
I don't know. They just didn't care, some say.
Do you think they wanted to get sick from what might have been on the vegetables?
No, they all agree.
Okay, she says. They must have thought it was safe.

I washed off my tomato because it was dirty and had been outside.
And I tasted the sweetness of the fresh tomato, Keveon says.
Ms. Caroline says she probably would have washed off hers too
and knows the Sousa garden tomato tastes far superior to what we usually find in supermarkets.

Speaking of tomatoes, did the garden have the ingredients
of a meal? Like a salad. Did it have lettuce, tomato, and carrots?,
Ms. Caroline asks.
Yes.
What kind of lettuce was there?
What do you mean? Is there more than one type of lettuce?
Actually, yes there is.
Mr. Xavier was on his way out of the room, but stops in his tracks, with a big smile
to back up Ms. Caroline's claim that there's more than one type of lettuce.
There's iceberg, field greens, butter lettuce, he and Ms. Caroline point out.
What! They put butter on lettuce?
Everybody laughs.
No, it's a type. Smooth to the touch, like butter. So soft and smooth,
it feels like it could melt in your hand.

Have you ever been to a garden like the one at Sousa?, Ms. Caroline asks.
No. I've never been to a garden like the one at Sousa, two people say.
I have been to a garden; once here (at Anacostia High School) and once at Kramer Middle School.
I want to plant a garden in my grandmother's backyard, Dewand says.

Before leaving, Erica recalls, they planted beets, melons, and basil seedlings
and watered all the newly planted plants.

One thing I like about the gardens is that, by planting them, you are actually doing something to better the world. I didn't mind shoveling holes so that we could plant more seedlings and make it better for the Earth, Dre writes.

Ms. Caroline had asked them earlier to share in writing what they felt or touched
when they were in the garden.
"I felt the stump of the tree that I sat on," Keveon says about
what his body physically felt and touched.
Turns out the garden touched his mind and his soul, too.
"I loved how calming it felt, being behind Sousa with no extra people. Just nature," he writes.
He seems to speak for most of the group, and the world.

The Day I Lifted My Voice in an Environmental Choir

by Miguel Zarate, College Intern

On a hot day in late June, I stroll into the UDC Student Center, ready to assist as a college intern for Conservation Nation in the UDC-DOI Justice 40 summer internship. The refreshingly cool interior houses a program that will engage Anacostia High School students in the environment and literacy. It feels daunting being here. I've worked with younger children as a swim coach, but I don't have much experience teaching concepts like this. I set my eyes on the large glass windows that look out at the city. I scan the round tables, where about a dozen students sit.

Each student has things that distinguish them – colorful or dark clothing, hair color and styles, the way they sit – some head up straight, others eyes cast down – but there is one uniting piece.
They all have a passion for nature and how they can make change in the world they're growing up in. I didn't grow up in DC, but I attended college nearby in College Park, MD. Occasionally, I would take runs in Anacostia. The emerald leaves lushly adorning the trees and the reflection of the sky on the river, which flows alongside the meandering trails, are what make me love the area so much. I can feel the love the students have for their home and the need to protect it.

I see that the group is filling in cards for a game of vocabulary "BINGO." Roaming the room is a woman ticking off words to jot down on the card, table by table. This woman, Author Caroline Brewer, an environmentalist and literacy consultant for the Anacostia program in partnership with Conservation Nation, UDC, and DOI, is extracting vocabulary from a picture book. It's called *Farmer Will Allen and the Growing Table*. Allen is the urban gardening legend behind the non-profit, Growing Power, and a MacArthur "Genius" award winner. He is also a 6'7" tall former pro basketball player.

Allen's parents were sharecroppers, meaning they worked for little pay on somebody's else's farm for a living. Sharecropping is a legacy of slavery. His parents migrated to this area and raised him just a few miles from UDC, in Rockville, MD. Allen's mother made meals with the fruits and vegetables from their garden here. After his pro career overseas, Allen settled in Milwaukee and started pioneering strategies for urban agriculture.

Early on, as Ms. Brewer shares vocabulary, some of the students mumble among each other and don't seem focused. Then everything changes as she begins to read. Her voice gets louder, booming at times, and changes in tone with Allen's story, rhythmically, as she invites students to echo phrases, sometimes catching them off guard, making them smile, taking them on a literary thrill ride. Like a garden of voices, their words grow from quiet, almost hushed, to strong and powerful speech, in sync, like a choir. It was incredible to witness her ability as a dynamic storyteller to involve the students.

Eventually, Ms. Brewer passes a book to me, inviting me to read. The artwork is captivating, and with the students' eyes on me, I feel a weight on my shoulders. I project my voice, narrating Allen's many triumphs as he transforms urban landscapes into fertile farmlands --something the students learn more about first-hand by visiting UDC's rooftop garden and others – after this rhythmic introduction.

As Will Allen brought fresh fruits and vegetables to the tables of Milwaukee, and eventually the world, Ms. Brewer brings her stories, and the stories of others, with uncharacteristic enthusiasm to teaching. With her guidance, bit by bit, my anxiety turned into confidence. Little did I know, this would be the start of not just an internship, but a journey, working with this author/educator and the high-schoolers.

I can't be more grateful to be a part of it.

In the Hydroponics Lab, Food Systems and Security are on the Menu
by Jacob Campbell

The Summer Youth Employment Program at Anacostia High-School has been a culmination of reading, writing, field trips, interviews, indoor hydroponics, and outdoor garden bed experiences. We also created a community asset map that identifies assets and the lack thereof. Students have interacted and learned from professionals across many sectors.

The University of the District of Columbia UDC has deployed large-and small-scale hydroponic systems to the LAB at Anacostia High School, which was established in 2022.

UDC Intern Olivia Howard led a seed propagation demonstration which highlighted the importance of correctly germinating seeds indoors and how it increases germination percentages and allows us to use the power of hydroponics to prepare larger crops for transplantation outdoors. We also talked about how youth can use these tools and skills to dispute current food systems and be environmental stewards while growing and distributing fresh produce that is nutrient-rich and calorically-dense.

The students worked in pairs with a variety of lettuces. They then placed them onto the large 36 grow site hydroponics system. One week later, they were able to return and see a 95% germination rate, which excited and encouraged them.

The following week, UDC interns Danielle Simmons, Olivia Howard, Tolu Adetosoye, and Allen Muir led two field trips. The first trip took the students to Kramer Middle School Garden where they were able to see how much food can be produced in small outdoor spaces. They all had chances to plant jalapeños, tomatoes, squash, and basil.

We also talked about how school and community gardens can have a large impact on food availability and food equity by putting the power of food production into the hands of the community. They were able to discuss large food hubs in the district and other ways people can grow food in their own small spaces. The second field trip was to a Sousa Middle School Garden where the students planted beets, basil, peppers, and flowers. At Sousa, some of the students tried freshly picked tomatoes and kale. We talked about taste profiles and taste sensations, and how they differ depending on how and where the food is produced.

Finally, to tie it all together, Alexandra, a nutrition specialist from Giant Foods, came and gave a presentation on food security, food deserts, and how personal food and snack choices not only impact our health and well-being, but the environment around us and the people and animals that share our ecosystems. We ended with a salad-making demonstration and taste test. The kale, cucumbers, basil, tomatoes were all harvested from the middle school gardens. Students seem eager to learn more. They said they'd like to try these types of things at home, and start talking to friends, family, and community members about the importance of food equity and security.

All Day with the EPA

All Day with the EPA
Contributors: Erica Doughty, Dearontre Daise, Keveon Graves, NeKaeyla Roach
Arranged by: Caroline Brewer

I hated
the old elevators,
the endless lonely hallways,
the small room.

The building smelled old.

I learned
about new career opportunities,
in areas such as spokespeople and tech.
I liked
the designs of the elevators;
reminded me of older lobbies from 1980s TV shows.
I got to see
a room fully dedicated to technology,
with computers and TV's everywhere,
where they track environmentally dangerous activities.

We heard
from professionals in the field -
a few engineers, an environmental enforcement officer,
an emergency response team member, and other scientists.
We sat
in this high security room,
located in the basement of the building.
The staff appeared relaxed.

One thing I learned when we went to the EPA is that
they record the oil spills. It's a global thing.
Turns out a Black man, John Francis, the Planetwalker,
helped federal agencies figure out how to analyze oil spills
after spending 20 years protesting oil spills
by refusing to ride in vehicles; instead he walked
or rode his bike everywhere, for thousands of miles
across the United States and other countries.

We met
with staff that had been handling the chemical spill in Ohio.
Most of their investigation had been finished
and they were looking into the long-term effects.

Another thing that was interesting
was learning more about water runoff,
the stuff on roofs,
the bacteria, dog poop, and urine on the ground,
and how it gets into our water.

I liked how they were asking what can they do
to have better exposure among the youth.
Interestingly, the man leading the tour started at the EPA
as an intern. And the woman helping with the tour
is now an intern.

I liked how they asked us what they do could better.
We told them we need more resources in Wards 7 and 8
to help with our water problems.
Some women said there was a time when from miles away
they could smell poop from the river.
They said now the smell is gone;
you can see through the water; see fish swimming.
They said the water quality is better than ever.

After going to the EPA, I felt inspired.
I've always wanted to do something specific to the environment.
I enjoyed hearing from the EPA Criminal Investigations Division.
I grew to love the EPA and their work.
It feels like a new career I could pursue.

I just wish
that we had chances to learn about more things like this.

CHAPTER 5

If I Were

We practiced writing personification poems inspired by the picture book, *If I Were a Tree* by Andrea Zimmerman and Illustrated by Jing Jing Tsong. The students were impressed by the ways in which the writer tapped into her five senses to bring the experiences of trees to life. An example: *"If I were a tree, I know what I'd feel. The warmth of the sun, and squirrels on the run. The climbing of boots, and worms by my roots."*

If I Were an Alligator
by Jeremiah Wright

If I were an alligator, I know what I would see:
My prey, dirty logs, tall weeds and swampy trees.

If I were an alligator, I know what I would hear:
Fish splashing, crickets chirping, and birds singing in my ears.

If I were an alligator, I know what I would smell:
Chemicals in the water helping me find my food,
as well as a ringing bell.

If I were an alligator, I know what I would love:
Dry land, rough fish, elderberries, and fresh air from above.

If I Were a Robin
by DeMirio Wimbush

If I were a robin, I know what I would hear:
Gunshots in Anacostia that sound like fireworks.
The pops feel so near.
I flap my wings to fly
to the closest tree
and recover from my fears.

If I were a robin, I know what I would see:
The brown Anacostia River flowing beneath me.
I'd also see kids wild and free,
trying to playfully capture me.

If I were a robin, I know what I would smell:
Turns out my receptors are greatly reduced,
meaning we songbirds don't smell very well.

If I were a robin, I know what I would taste:
worms, spiders, berries, and all outdoors
crashing against my beak.

If I were a robin, I know what I would touch:
water to clean my wings and the branches of trees
that balance me as I clutch.

If I Were an Eagle
by Dearontre (Dre) Daise

If I were an eagle, I know what I would see:
fish, insects, land, and big and tall trees

If I were an eagle, I know what I would hear:
humans, vehicles, falcons, and water that's always near

If I were an eagle, I know what I would taste:
bass, salmon, insects, worms, and jackrabbits I have to chase

If I were an eagle, I know what I would love:
flying high up in the sky,
and the wild spaces of my life,

which give me a perpetual shove.

If I Were a Blue Jay
by Kahri Borum

If I were a blue jay, I know what I would see everyday:
Gardens, groves, woods, and towns – I hope my habitat never decays!

If I were a blue jay, I know where I would lay:
In a bulky cup made of twigs, grass, moss, bark strips, and mud.
In my nest, I always get my way.

If I were a blue jay, I know what I would eat:
beetles, grasshoppers, caterpillars, and spiders.
They make my diet complete.

If I Were a Leech
by Keveon Graves

If I were a leech, I would taste the blood from my prey
both tomorrow and today
If I were a leech, I would taste the sliminess of fish eggs
as well as the stiff
textures of warm legs

I would taste the skin of a snake
while continuing to eat even as it starts to shake
The more I eat, the more I taste,
clearing out my food with very great haste

If I were a leech, I would feel my victim's bottom lip
stay on as long as I can, even if it plans to rip
I would feel climbing up a tree,
hanging from branches shaped like the letter "C"

I would feel myself sliding across the ground
maybe even crawl if I really need to get around
I would feel slimy wet skin
doing so many things that I can't help
but to sin

If I were a leech, I would love to keep taking blood
Doesn't matter who it is, it always feels good
Taking too much puts me in a mood
Don't ever forget that it's technically my food

I would love to slowly munch on worms
I break them in fours like they're high school terms
I would also love to sit on a table
But I would much rather leech onto a cable

If I were a leech, I would smell my next victim
I would be able to resist sticking it to them
I would be able to smell their warm soul
It makes me want to put them in a bowl

I would smell the grass and trees around me
Don't look for innocence, as it's your doom you will see
I would smell the rain in the air
I walk, they run, just so they think things are fair.

If I Were a Birdwing Butterfly
by Nekaeyla Roach

If I were a birdwing butterfly, I'd see water swooshing back and forth.
If I were a birdwing butterfly, I'd fly myself way up north.
Being a birdwing butterfly,
I would hear low pitch sounds to help me detect
the flapping of vicious bird wings
trying to crash-land on my neck – and eat me!

If I were a birdwing butterfly, I know what I would sense:
the aroma of flowers from miles away,
thanks to antennae that are receptor-dense.
And did I forget to mention,
since I am the biggest butterfly in the world
I would love landing on a nice wooden fence.

Since my family and I don't have tongues,
most of our tastebuds are focused on our feet.
Which means I can't forget to mention,
that I know what I would love to eat:
nectar, because to me, it's oh, so sweet.

If I were a birdwing butterfly, I know what I would love:
how my wings spread so beautifully -
up to 11 inches wide, and delicate -
so handle me with kid gloves.

And then there's my tranquil color
that reminds me of the sky.
Remember to treat me well and protect me
because the Queen Alexandra species
is an endangered birdwing butterfly.

If I Were a Gentoo Penguin
by Erica Doughty

If I were a gentoo penguin, I know what I would see:
snow, ice, water, and mountains,
all around and underneath me.

If I were a gentoo penguin, I know what I would hear:
splashing water, fish jumping,
baby penguins making noise in my ear.

If I were a gentoo penguin, I know what I would smell:
fish and fish blood, the saltiness of sea life in my 'hood.

If I were a gentoo penguin, I know what I would be:
the faster swimmer in the bird kingdom;
so hurry if you plan to catch me;
I'll be flying 20 mph through the chilly waters
of the deep blue sea.
I'll be diving up to 450 times a day,

so I can feed my family.

If I Were a Red Fox
by Royana Easterling

If I were a red fox, I know what I would see:
grass to hide and find food and the chance to explore trees.

If I were a red fox, I know what I would hear:
other animals in the forest, the river flowing,
and trees moving with the wind.

If I were a red fox, I know what I would taste:
the juiciness of berries, rabbits, and rodents I eat with haste.

If I were a red fox, I know what I would touch:
grass that I walk and run on so much.

If I were a red fox, I know what I would be:
an animal with a reddish coat, black legs,
and a long, white-tipped tail roaming freely.

If I Were a Crocodile
by Dewand Hemsley

If I were a crocodile, I know what I would see: fish, people, swamps, and trees.
If I were a crocodile, I know what I would be:
I'd be an animal with powerful jaws, sharp, cone-shaped teeth,
rough, scaly skin, and clawed webbed feet.
If I were a crocodile I would have excellent ears.
I would hear piercing sounds that humans can't hear.
If I were a crocodile I would smell animal carcasses from far away,
whether on land or in the water, night and day.

CHAPTER 6

Anacostia

If I Were the Anacostia River
by Keveon Graves, Jeremiah Wright, Kahri Borum, Marcus Williams, Dewand Hemsley, Dearontre Daise, DeMirio Wimbush, Germaine Williams, NeKaeyla Roach, and Royana Easterling

If I were the Anacostia River, I know what I would see:
trash, bass, Carolina wrens and
skinny branches that have fallen from trees

If I were the Anacostia River, I know what I would hear:
birds chirping, ducks quacking, cars roaring,
and wind blowing in my ear

If I were the Anacostia River, I know what I would smell:
gas from vehicles mixed with mallow flowers,
poke weed and milkweed and berry bushes,
like those you might find in a dell

If I were the Anacostia River, I know what I would know:
paddle boards, kayaks, and canoes enjoy my flow
I'm 8.4 miles long and up to 15 feet deep
My name comes from the Nacotchtank People
I get my water from many creeks

If I were the Anacostia River, I know what I would love:
the green of the trees,
clean water, less pollution,
more wildlife and fish that people can eat,
and the peace symbolized by the dove

Thanks to the staff of the Bladensburg Waterfront Park for the riverboat tour that gave us such beautiful views of the Anacostia.

Anacostia Park Would Be Sweeter, If Development Hadn't Wiped Out the Honeysuckle

by Danielle Simmons, Anacostia Ambassador

When I was asked to share all the edible plants, fruits and herbs that grow East of the River, I smiled. Within seconds, I knew what I would share first.

I always wanted to tell the special story of the native honeysuckle; a story that began when I was a child. Seeing the blooms marked the first signs of summer and the school year being near its end. The vines would hang loosely from the bush onto the gates creating an arch over the sidewalk. During my morning walks to school, I would pluck them, one by one, and tilt my head back far as it could go to enjoy the squeezed nectar dropping like raindrops. There was less than a pea-sized amount in each petal, yet each was enormously fragrant and sweet. Today, seeing a native honey suckle tree in D.C. is impossible. They have all been wiped out due to development.

I spent my childhood East of the River, and the dense forests and Anacostia Park are where I enjoyed hanging out – a lot. I don't remember my first encounter with blackberries, but it was probably while playing in the forests chasing lightning bugs, also known as fireflies. They have always been one of my favorite things to forage midsummer, even before I knew foraging was a thing.

Berry bushes grow along the edge of Anacostia Park, stretching miles, and covering many parts of D.C. In season, the berries start out bright red and eventually turn a deep violet, signifying their ripeness. I eat them straight from the bush, although I should consider washing them. My logic is: what if we operated in the mind-space of how nature intended us to enjoy her bounty? However, it's important to never confuse the blackberries with the red "bird berries" that grow wild on the ground with the violets and clovers. They are poisonous.

Burdock, chamomile, echinacea and dandelions are all native edible plants and flowers East of the River. Mallows too! Mallows grow on the Anacostia riverbanksand are in full bloom throughout summer. Marshmallows are made from the mallow plant (athaea officinalis) that grows wild in marshes. Burdock grows wild in a particular area of Oxon Run. Their season for harvest is at the beginning of fall. The root is traditionally used to make tea.

Anacostia is not only full of sweet things to eat. It's full of sweet memories. For future generations, may we fight to keep it that way.

Danielle Simmons is a native Washingtonian and founder of We Care DC, an environmental agency that is committed to the preservation of Earth and its natural resources, with an emphasis on urban agriculture, wildlife habitat conservation, and the implementation of green infrastructure. She also is currently a student at CAUSES (College of Agriculture Urban Sustainability and Environmental Sciences) and serving as an environmental justice ambassador with the Department of Interior in partnership with UDC.

CHAPTER 7

Getting Around with Xavier Brown: A Praise Poem

by Caroline Brewer, with Kahri Borum, Dearontre (Dre) Daise, Alexis Allen, Erica Doughty, and Danielle Simmons

From food apartheid,
he won't let you hide
For agroecology,
he makes no apology
For climate justice,
is his fight
To just transitions,
he brings the light

This poem is singing the praises
of a man whose work ethic amazes
We praise the ancestors
for Anacostia Ambassador Xavier Brown

For his walks with us
For his talks with us
His calls to awaken and awaken all the good stuff in us

For his listening to us and hearing us
For his quiet, behind-the-scenes incessant cheering for us
For his spirit-lifting
For his advice-gifting

For crossing busy roads for us
For carrying heavy loads for us
For sitting with us
Being tough, at times, with us
But never rough

For laboring with us
For laughing with us
For reading to us
For seeding us - a better future

We praise the ancestors for Xavier Brown
For him being earth, wind, fire, water, and air to us
For him taking the time to help repair us

For his imagination, for his dedication,
for his peace-be-still, no ways tired exemplification

We praise the ancestors for Xavier Brown

Working with Mr. Xavier has been fun. I like how he has patience with us and doesn't let us do the bare minimum. What I appreciate most about Mr. Xavier is that he gave us the opportunity to be in this program, and he also makes sure we eat good. – Alexis Allen

One thing I learned working with Mr. Xavier that he is an outgoing person and someone you can depend on. I appreciate the new knowledge he exposed me to and how he helped me have a better understanding of our environment. – Dearontre (Dre) Daise

He's patient and kind. Also, easy to work with. – Danielle Simmons

Getting around, uptown, downtown,
in the park, on the river, in the gardens, at school, being cool,
on the UDC campus, sitting down to eat, enjoying treats,
with Mr. Brown – it's been a pleasure and a privilege,
one of the rarest ever to be found

We praise the ancestors for Xavier Brown

CHAPTER 8

The Thing About Fear

The Thing About Fear
by Caroline Brewer

This chapter, and the following essays on *If I Were*, were inspired by Eric-Shabazz Larkin's picture book, *The Thing About Bees: A Love Letter*. Shabazz's love letter is to his sons. He grew up fearing bees and after he learned about their benefits to our ecosystem, including human food systems, he promised himself that he wouldn't pass on his fear to his boys.

I've read Shabazz's letter to many audiences, and every group, including our Anacostia students, has responded with aahs of appreciation, especially for his sweet little twist at the end. Mr. Xavier did us the favor of reading the book, as we echoed it back to him. The students and I followed up by exploring what we knew about bees, and what we had in common with them. One of their responses was that bees had wings, and we do too, when we're practicing being angels. I loved that!

So the assignment for this chapter was to do two things: Write a haiku about bees, and a short piece on wildlife that are commonly feared by humans. They were to tell us the characteristics of the wildlife, what value they bring to the planet, and what we can do to overcome the sense of terror and dread we have when we see them or even hear their names mentioned.

The thing about fear, many authorities have observed, is that's it's paralyzing, polarizing, and a thief. It steals joy and happiness, a sense of peace, and possibilities. And at its worst, fear steals livelihoods and lives. It robs us of relationships and our connections to our global family;
to all that's wild and wonderful, and absolutely necessary for us to thrive and be fully human.

This is a chapter, as you might by now suspect, that's about more than fear of animals or poisonous plants. It's about our fear of each other, whoever the other might be, and of obstacles, wherever they might emerge.

With *Through My Anacostia Eyes*, the students gained opportunities to face and confront all sorts of fears, including the fear of letting what they felt deep inside spill out on the page. And if we adults were wise, we followed in the students' footsteps. Bless them for being leaders.

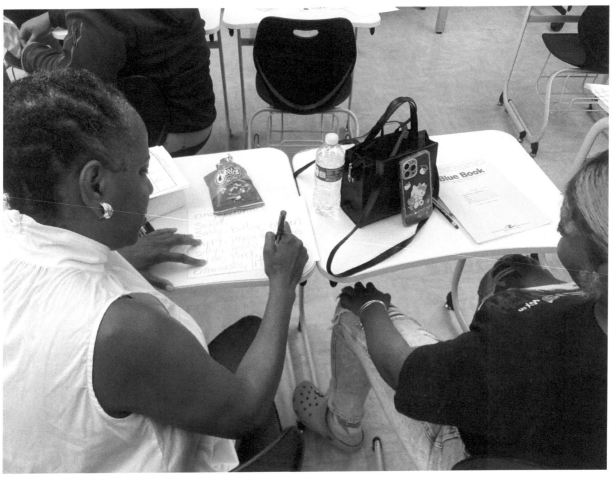

The Thing About Bees
(Group Haiku – Contributors Dewand Hemsley, Germane Williams, Keveon Graves)

Some bees sting, some don't
When they attack, they fight back
Bumblees don't sting

The Thing About Humble Bees
by Germaine Williams

Humble bumble bee
brings pollen from apple tree
to make his honey

The Thing About Bees; No Debate
by Keveon Graves

New homes bees create
No debate; humans relate
Bees do pollinate

The Thing About Bees Buzzing
by Dearontre Daise

Buzzing in the air
Nature's workers, small and fair
Busy bees, take care

The Thing About Hornets
by Dewand Hemsley

Hornets are big and sting
They protect their queen with attacks
They sting and don't die

The Thing About Copperhead Snakes
by DeMirio Wimbush

The thing about copperhead snakes is that they are slithery, mysterious, venomous, and long.
The longer their bodies are, the longer their fangs are.
Although they are venomous, their bites are rarely fatal.

Copperhead snakes are good for controlling pests.
Their skin is used to make decorative belts and purses.

Copperhead snakes can breed every year like us.
And like humans, they can consume twice their body weight in a year.
We can overcome our fears of snakes by learning about them.

The Thing About Wolves
by Dewand Hemsley

In my research, I learned that the thing about wolves is they communicate through body language, such as scent marking, barking growing, howling. They are leaders and team workers.

Alpha wolves make decisions and control the pack, like human parents. For this reason, wolves are described as a "keystone species." Their presence is vital to maintaining the health, structure and balance of ecosystems.

The Thing About Grizzly Bears
by Dearontre (Dre) Daise

This is a love letter to the world about grizzly bears.
The internet says that grizzly bears have strong jaws and
long, sharp claws that they use for digging, climbing,
and catching prey. It goes on to say that a swipe from a grizzly's paw
can cause serious injuries or even be fatal to humans.
That's why most humans, rightly, are afraid of them.

Grizzly bears used to live all across America but fear of them,
hunting, and destroying their habitat reduced their numbers dramatically.
They are now a threatened species and only live in the upper Northwest.

I read that grizzly bears control the salmon populations.
They keep deer moving so they don't overgraze
(and eat the stuff other animals and humans need to live).
The berries grizzlies eat leave seeds and fertilizer in their poop and that helps the ecosystem.

Somebody wrote that a characteristic of grizzly bears is
that they triumph over difficulties, proving they have an indomitable spirit.
"In Native American lore, the grizzly bear is a sacred animal, often seen as a spiritual guide or totem,
representing strength, courage, and wisdom," according to spiritualdesk.com

Think about that the next time you think about what you fear, and why,
and how knowing more about the grizzly can help you overcome your fears.

The Thing About Crocodiles
by Keveon Graves

I do not have a general fear of any of the animals we listed, but one of my favorite animals from the bunch is the crocodile.

From websites I visited, I learned that the biggest reptile on the planet is the saltwater crocodile, up to 20.7 feet in length. The have a bite force of about 3700 pounds per square inch, and can weigh up to 3,300 pounds. The saltwater crocodile inhabits coastal brackish mangrove swamps, river deltas, and freshwater rivers from India's east coast. They mainly eat fish, turtles, and wild buffalo, however, they have no problem eating humans. The only other crocodile with humans really on their diet is the Nile crocodile.

Crocodiles, as a whole species, are environment protectors. During the dry seasons, they prevent land animals from using or eating from the water. This protects aquatic life and systems. Protecting and restoring crocodile habitats benefits people by creating clean water and healthy fish supplies.

CHAPTER 9

Bird Brother

Bird Brother and Agnes

Contributors: NeKaeyla Roach, Keveon Graves, Dewand Hemsley, Dearontre Daise, and Germaine Williams, plus Xavier Brown

Not long after most of us arrived, Mr. Xavier escorted us from the classroom to the school's front steps. Mr. Rodney Stotts, known as Bird Brother, was waiting. Mr. Rodney is a Master Falconer, one of only a few Black falconers in the country. He said he drove four hours from his home outside Richmond, Virginia to meet us. We were impressed and grateful he drove that far to see us. Mr. Xavier said Mr. Rodney made the sacrifice to come because they're friends, and so much about what happens in this program, and in life, is about relationships.

Mr. Rodney pulled out a bird with fluffy feathers and wide wings. The wings were maybe two feet wide on each side, dark brown and black, and white on the edges. We learned he was holding a female Harris's Hawk. He said female hawks are 30-40 percent bigger than male hawks. Male hawks fly faster to hunt food for females and their babies. Male hawks are the only birds of prey that hunt in pairs to protect themselves from other birds of prey.

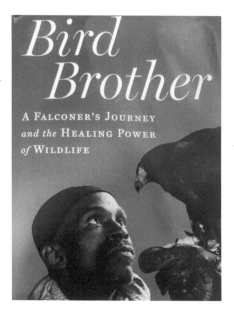

Mr. Rodney pulled the hawk from a black box the size of a two-drawer file cabinet. "When he brought out the hawk, I started thinking of Sky (the eagle at Earth Conservation Corps) because of the excited way it acted when it saw people," Keveon said.

The hawk tried to fly away, then ruffled her feathers, which Mr. Rodney told us they do when they feel comfortable around people. "I liked how they had a bond," NeKaeyla said. "Everything he told Agnes (the hawk) to do, she did... She tried to walk up his arm and he told her to stop, and she did. Told her she knew better than to do that."

Mr. Rodney said a woman named Agnes Nixon bought him the hawk many years ago. Agnes Nixon used to write soap operas for a living. Only two people in our group have heard of soap operas. He said he names all of his animals after loved ones who have passed away, like his son, his mother, and Agnes Nixon. He has a seven-acre farm, something of an animal sanctuary, Mr. Xavier said. We remembered three horses, six dogs, 18 rabbits, two goats, three hawks, but couldn't remember the other animals – there were so many.

He told us hawks don't have a sense of smell, but they have great vision. We noticed that while Agnes was sitting on his arm, she would track something with her eyes like she was ready to go after it. We also noticed that the other birds in the area started to get loud and noisy as soon as Agnes flew out of the box. It seemed like they were warning each other that a bird of prey was in the neighborhood. That was deep.

Early on in his book, called Bird Brother, Mr. Rodney said he learned quickly that "a human relationship with anything wild would require three things: love, patience, and respect...Once we understand the

*A falconer practices the ancient art of training and hunting with falcons and other birds of prey. Today, falconry is practiced both for conservation purposes, such as raptor rehabilitation and population management, as well as for recreational purposes. -careerexplorer.com

Matthew Henson Earth Conservation Corps Center and John Wood

The UDC-DOI Justice 40 Summer Internship students visited the Matthew Henson Earth Conservation Corps Center (ECC) and met Field Director John Wood. John introduced students to Devon, a barn owl, and Sky, an eagle. He spoke about the powerful work of ECC, its founding corps member Bird Brother Rodney Stotts, and the center's namesake, Explorer Matthew Henson.

According to its website: Earth Conservation Corps empowers youth from stressed communities through service learning, habitat restoration, and environmental education. Across 30 years, our young volunteers have demonstrated that restoring habitats, assisting field biologists and caring for a raptor ambassador is transformative experience that inspires a lifelong connection to nature and reconnection to self.

John Wood is pictured here holding Devon, a barn owl.

John Wood is the Field Director for Earth Conservation Corps. He spent seven years going through eight different ranks to become an Eagle Scout. Growing up, he had a passion for nature and the environment. He started out as an Earth Conservation Corps AmeriCorps member doing 900 hours from 2018-2019, before joining the ECC staff full-time.

He has been a part of handling all the raptors and raptor programming for the past three years and was promoted to Field Director to begin leading all programming within the past year. He now cares for all of our animals, takes care of both our DC campuses, and hosts programs that we do with various DC partners including: Youth Creative Change, Anacostia River Keepers, podcast groups, and various schools in the DC area, shared Sonora Burn, Program Manager, ECC.

A Salute to Matthew Henson
by Miguel Zarate

Matthew Alexander Henson was an African American explorer born in Charles County (Nanjemoy), Maryland on August 8th, 1866, shortly after the abolition of slavery. However, his parents had been born free and he became one of the first African Americans, that we know of, to roam the world freely. Both of his parents died by the time he was 11.

At age 12, Henson walked from DC to Baltimore and signed up to work on the ship the *Katie Hines*, where Captain Childs was the skipper.

Childs taught Henson reading, writing, Math, geography, and navigation. They traveled to Africa, Asia, and Europe.

At the age of 21, Childs died and Henson left the *Katie Hines*. For a while he lived in D.C. as a shop clerk. Eventually, he met Navy Corps of Engineers Officer Robert Peary, who hired him as a valet, or personal attendant. But Henson quickly demonstrated he was capable of a lot more.

The two worked together on expeditions around the world. Peary was the man working with the public while Henson worked behind-the-scenes. Henson built and maintained their sleds, learned the Inuit language of people living in the Artic, and surveyed the land they were to travel.

Henson's relationship with the Inuit was critical to their success. His proficiency as a sailor and explorer rivaled or exceeded other experts they worked with.

In 1908, the men were in their 40s, and agreed on one last expedition to the North Pole. Starvation and extreme cold were constant threats. Not enough food to go around and below zero temperatures were guarantees that some explorers would meet with death.

After several attempts, on April 6, 1909, Henson, Peary, and four Inuit men -- Ooqueah, Ootah, Egingwah, Seegloo – reached the North Pole. Technically Henson was first, but because he was Black and didn't have Peary's connections to the Navy and other institutions, Peary was, for decades, credited with the accomplishment. Henson and the Inuit men would finally receive recognition in 1937. Nearly 100 years later, the word is still spreading.

Henson's pioneering spirit is a foundation for the work of the Matthew Henson Earth Conservation Corps Center (ECC) in Washington, D.C.

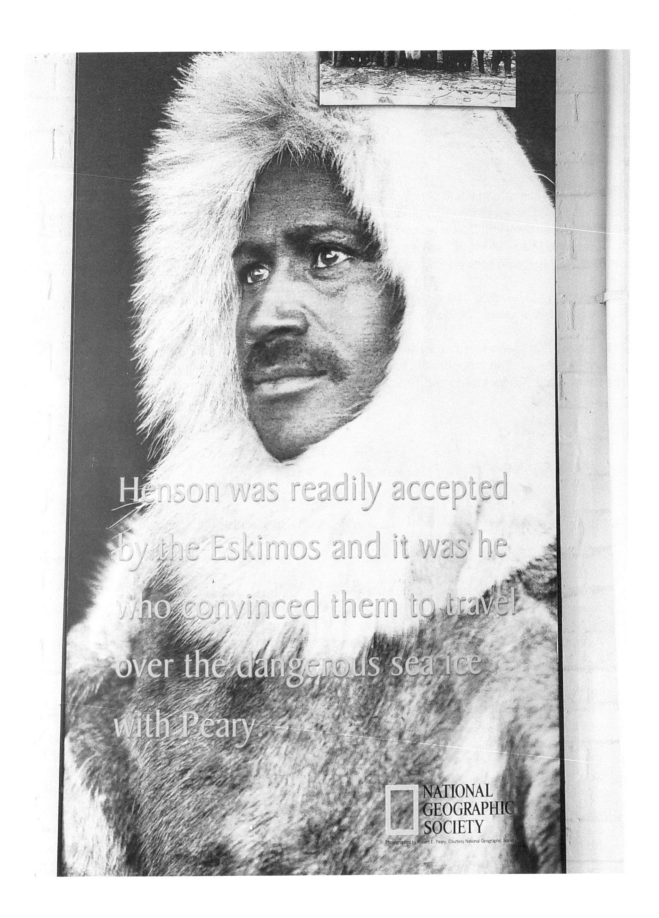

Henson was readily accepted by the Eskimos and it was he who convinced them to travel over the dangerous sea ice with Peary.

NATIONAL
GEOGRAPHIC
SOCIETY

Photographed by Robert E. Peary, Courtesy National Geographic Society

CHAPTER 10

DC Water Reflections

DC WATER
by Dearontre (Dre) Daise

DC Water was something I didn't know much about. I learned that the headquarters was basically designed so that it never would flood at a certain water level; that they estimated this many years in advance. When they told us the reason the building was shaped like that, "curvilinear, S-shaped, on the Anacostia River, meant to 'evoke the fluidity of the water,' " according to Architecture Magazine, I was shocked because they were so ahead of the game.

I also learned the building next door, the Main Pumping Station, was built in the early 1900s. The architecture is the same. They just added new machines.

After leaving, I still wondered how deep the tunnels were because they mentioned that the tunnels are under the river. The thought of that, to me, is crazy. After getting back to school, I looked it up. The tunnels are 120 feet deep and 12,500 feet long.

At DC Water, Views from the Rooftop and Down Low
by Stephen Akyereko, Community Affairs Specialist, DC Water

During the headquarters tour, Anacostia Summer Internship students were treated to:

- The history of the DC Water sewer system, the main pumping station, and the O street pumping station locations
- A tour of the new building location, built above the O Street station
- A review of the new building structure and light features
- À review of the wastewater recovery energy system that helps power temperature controls
- A review of the DC water drinking source and distribution network and filtration process
- A review of Wastewater network, filtration process, and byproducts (Bloom)

During the Main Pumping Station Tour, students:

- Got brief history of the main pumping station
- Saw the pumps and various sizes
- Saw the control room and 24-hour-grid watch of clean and wastewater networks
- Saw the wastewater filter room (Clogged with "flushable" wipes)

During lunch:

- Students saw the DC Water rooftop, how we collect rainwater to redistribute it, along with the green roof. They also got to enjoy a special view of the city.

62

CHAPTER 11

Kenilworth Aquatic Gardens Tour

Kenilworth Aquatic Gardens

National Park Service
U.S. Department of Interior

1986-2016

Walter McDowney grew up around the corner from Kenilworth Aquatic Gardens at Kenilworth Courts. He loved exploring the outdoors and found inspiration in nature. His knowledge of nature caught the attention of park rangers and soon Walter became "Ranger Mac" and worked in the National Park Service for over 30 years. Ranger Mac created the Junior Ranger program at the gardens and was passionate about getting youth in the area involved in the outdoors. He organized camping trips and outdoor adventures for junior rangers, inspiring a new generation of environmental enthusiasts.

Printed in the USA
CPSIA information can be obtained
at www.ICGtesting.com
LVHW071652081123
763414LV00003B/16